Cosmic Cow

Pie...

Connecting

the Dots

Reviews

"Cosmic Cow Pie is the practical and amusing information we all need. Rarely do you find a book that gives sound business advice as well as pointers for how to live your life. Riley's book combines helpful principles plus a healthy dose of common sense. A must for every individual's compendium of rules to live by! Riley's got her attitude on straight and her advice on HOT!"

Marcia Fine
Author, Speaker, Publisher,
Entrepreneur
Scottsdale, Arizona

"Absolutely delightful read! It is full of common sense and things you already know but put together in a new package. The book gives you ideas of how to reason and think through many problems. It helps 'join the dots' as we say in England."

Linda Binder
Former Arizona State Senator
District 3
Lake Havasu City, Arizona

"Cosmic Cow Pie... Connecting the Dots" was a fast, fun read... in fact what I learned will last me a lifetime. Carra provides practical applications to principles that will lead to success without stress. The stand alone chapters are a great reminder of not only how to avoid the cow pies of life but how to excel while you're on your journey."

Faith Barnard
Former TV Personality
Social Media and Network
Marketing Consultant
Sedona, Arizona

"Cosmic Cow Pie is a down-to-earth book that addresses how to handle the very complicated subject of life and all it may hand us or throw in our path. Carra Riley neatly and concisely "connected the dots" for us, using fourteen common sense principles that can be applied in almost any situation. There are terrific references, from famous lines in songs to great literary quotes, punctuating the already clear messages in each chapter. Dots connected – cosmic cow pies deflected! Thank you for a great read – and re-read!"

Theresa (Tea) Pennisi
Ever-aspiring model,
actress and artist
New York City, New York

"This book is a life-changing read. It allowed me to process what I've been through and defined what I need to do in order to make changes in my own life. It is very educational, heartwarming and a huge wake up call for me. I will be sharing it with my friends."

James Miller
Physical Therapy
Flagstaff, Arizona

"I just finished your book. It was fun. The 'I get it – I don't get it' chapter was the most thought provoking for me. That one seemed very new. To actually just give yourself permission to move on was pretty powerful stuff. I think there is something that everyone will be able to have an 'ah ha moment' when they read it."

Wendy Atkinson
Realtor, Investor, Golf Expert
Westminster, Colorado

"The book was a pleasure to read. I have volunteered for years and could relate to the Dr. Phil chapter. You made me laugh and I am sure many people can relate and will be helped by this delightful book!"

Valaida D'Alessio
MultiMedia Artist, Writer
Maui, Hawaii

"Each time I have read it, through your months of writing, it has inspired me, taught me, and made me re-think things in my life. What an awesome collection of life's helpers that we all need. You have it all together and presented so beautifully."

Jeri Evans
Top Producing Real Estate Broker
Re/Max Professionals
Highlands Ranch, Colorado

"Okay, I woke up at 4:30, read for a while, finally got up at 5:30, checked various e-mails, and decided to read the book. Yes, I love it! This year is the first one that hasn't been as much fun. I haven't really had a Plan B. I need to make some changes. Thanks."

Jacqui Jeffress
Infinity Real Estate Services
Boulder, Colorado

"I have to admit, I am not a reader, but this book kept my interest all the way through to the end. I took the chapters in Carra's book, applied the principles to my life, and came out a winner. It is back to the basics and SIMPLE to understand."

Sheri Roose
Artist/Business Owner
Lake Havasu City, Arizona

"Thank you, Carra, for guiding me away from stepping into too many Cosmic Cow Pies. I love your no nonsense, yet fun, way of putting things into perspective and giving me permission to live a SWSWSWN life."

Pamela Cendejas
Second Self Virtual Assistance
Lake Havasu City, Arizona

"Carra Riley really cuts through the crap! The Cosmic Cow Pie is a friendly little kick in the pants. A simple and exceptionally humorous reminder of the basic facts of day-to-day living. Thanks! I needed that."

Craig Roose
Set Decorator
Los Angeles, California

"The book reminded me of things I had forgotten and pointed out new principles to help me avoid some of life's Cosmic Cow Pies. Carra doesn't just write the words, she actually lives them which was important to me. This book will change your life."

John Panico
Article Authority Guru, Consultant
Atlanta, Georgia

About the Author

Carra Riley came in with a bang on July 4, 1953 and has been lighting things up ever since. Baby Boomer, wife, mother, daughter, stepdaughter, mother-in-law, grandmother, stepmother, stepsister, sister-in-law, daughter-in-law, great aunt, cousin, friend, teacher, investor, and entrepreneur: you name it, she's been it!

Carra has lived and worked in Denver/Boulder, Colorado; New York City, New York; Kansas City, Missouri; Lake Tahoe, California; Maui, Hawaii; Lake Havasu City and Mohave County, Arizona. She was a retail buyer, taught Merchandising at Colorado State University, and had a 30 year Real Estate Career in Colorado, Arizona, and Hawaii. Along with her husband, she also owned two retail businesses, Colorado's Incredible Machine in Estes Park, and

Tahoe's Incredible Machine in Lake Tahoe, California.

Riley led an eventful life growing up in a Denver, Colorado suburb. She rode her bike around the city, and in 4th grade sold "Carra's Cinnamon Suckers" on the playground at recess, doubling her money daily. For her recipe, please visit www.CosmicCowPie.com.

Carra has personally experienced success with all the diversity in her past. The experiences helped her navigate the **COSMIC COW PIE** and **CONNECT THE DOTS** of life. Her insight helps readers reduce anxiety in processing all the "asteroids" the universe throws out. The principles she shares are simple, powerful and life changing.

Look for the children's workbook entitled **COSMIC COW PIE... CONNECTING KIDS' DOTS** and her next book, **COSMIC COW PIE...SURVIVAL 101: RULES OF LIFE** at her website: www.CosmicCowPie.com.

For further information about Carra's books, CDs, and workshops, or to schedule her for a presentation or speaking engagement, please contact:

Carra Riley, Inc.

P. O. Box 922

Williams, AZ 86046

info@CarraRiley.com or www.CosmicCowPie.com or

Skype: Carra Riley   (skype name: cosmiccowpie)

Cosmic Cow Pie...

Connecting the Dots

Concepts you know framed in

easy to follow

principles

to help balance your life.

Carra Riley Press

Publisher's Cataloging-In-Publication Data (Prepared by The Donohue
Group, Inc.)

Riley, Carra.
    Cosmic cow pie-- . Connecting the dots : concepts you know framed in easy to
follow principles to help balance your life / [Carra Riley]. -- 1st ed.

    p. : ill. ; cm. -- (Cosmic cow pie)

    ISBN: 978-0-9841999-0-7

1. Conduct of life. 2. Life. 3. Happiness. I. Title.

BF637.C5 R55 2009
158

Cover Design and Artwork for Chapter 2, 8, 10, 15 by Jackie Dras
Artwork for Cover by Sheri Roose
Graphics by Dreamstime.com:

©Uladzimir Hryshcanka	Chapter 4
©Markarova Olga	Chapter 5
© Connie Larsen	Chapter 6
© John Takai	Chapter 7
©Raja Rc	Chapter 9
©Freud	Chapter 11
© Carolyne Pehora	Chapter 12
©Neonnyc	Chapter 13
©Tasosk	Chapter 14

Published by:
CR Press
P.O. Box 922
Williams, AZ 86046
First edition

Dedication

I have endless gratitude to my husband Tom and daughter Shae for putting up with my learning curve as I found my way to process the Cosmic Cow Pie of life. They were frequently casualties of my misdirected work anger and now they have been the catalysts to help me grow and find balance in my life. Thanks to Shannon, Kelly and Alex who have given me so many ideas, and to my grandsons Riley and Declan who asked me how much the book would cost when they found out I was writing and wanted to be the first to purchase it! To KC who was there with patience and encouragement all the way. To all who have inspired me, thanks for sharing the vision!

Table of Contents

Cosmic Cow Pie... Connecting the Dots

Introduction

Cosmic Cow Pie... Connecting the Dots

Without balance, everything seems out of control. Life seems like one continuous field of Cow Pies. For city dwellers, these are the presents left behind from cows in a field. Sometimes, it seems like the Universe overflows with cow pie after cow pie. This is the story of my life's lessons while dodging cow pies, during thirty years in the Real Estate business and along with my husband, raising a family. My life experiences have been exciting and compare to one amusement park ride after another. We seemed to be running from one adrenaline rush to the next, just getting through all the cow pies which came into the pathway, trying to get personal agendas intertwined with business goals. Our philosophy exemplified when the music stopped, we would have gone for all the brass rings that were out there and would have left no stone unturned. Plans were developed for the next event and decisions made on the fly. The only consolation was if they were wrong, we were flexible to change again. We always felt, at least, we were making forward progress. "Calm" and "peaceful" were not adjectives that described the flow of our daily events. We would get up in the morning, put on our flak jackets and run.

Once we stopped the running, got off the hamster wheel and started slowing down, we began to connect all of the important aspects in our lives, and we received a clearer image of how values in our lives were supposed to connect to one another. The picture became crystal-clear, like looking through a magnifying glass and seeing everything come together with balance.

I hope that this book will inspire you to modify your behavior on the quest for a balanced life as you learn to dodge the cow pies flying around in your universe using the 14 Principles identified. You will be able to connect the dots of values so your life reflects the clear focus of how you really want to live.

The principles expressed in this book can make a difference in how you process the "Cosmic Cow Pie" of life. It is all about how you respond to the cards dealt to you. It is how you play them and what you think to get your direction. Kenny Rogers sings a song about this concept: "Know when to hold 'em, know when to fold 'em, know when to walk away, know when to run." When you finally "Connect the Dots," you will be focused and balanced.

Many of the principles you will read are just a "reframing" of concepts you have heard before. They frame my real life experiences as a recovered Real Estate agent, after 30 years of running at maximum speed. I hope you will learn from the book and not have to make some of the painful mistakes I did. The concepts can help take the pit out of your stomach when bad things happen. You can pick yourself up by the bootstraps and move on. You can build a bridge and get over it! You can take that red wagon that you pull behind you with all your baggage and install a "dump button" on it. You will be on your way to life with the focus of a ninja, balanced to perfection.

For example, change is in the air! The government is bailing out financial institutions and many foreign companies are buying others. The government borrowed money to provide a "stimulus package" to the American public and all they could do was buy some gas and eat another couple weeks. Exactly what did America "pledge" as collateral for all these loans? Where will this all end and how do we connect all the economic "Cow Pies" flying around us?

Our lives will be different in the years ahead. We need to have the tools and be ready to adapt to the definite change taking place. The skills to Read, Think, and Reason are more important now than ever. Understanding how to CONNECT THE DOTS IN THE COSMIC COW PIE will enable you to weather the storm. You never know when your world is going to change and how you fit into the picture.

December 30, 2008...Denver Broncos coach Mike Shanahan was "kicked to the curb" by long time friend and Bronco owner, Pat Bowlen. Mike had $20 million left on his 3-year contract with a huge new home under construction and got the boot.

2008 was Mike's 14th season as head coach of the Denver Broncos, a franchise he had guided to two Super Bowl victories, three conference championship game appearances, seven postseason berths, and nine winning seasons. His achievements as Denver's head coach starting on Jan. 31, 1995 had helped position the 49-year-old franchise among the most successful and highly regarded in all of professional sports.

In the 2008 NFL season, the Broncos had a three game lead to win the Division at the end of the season. They only had to win one additional game to make the NFL playoffs.

The Broncos did not win any of the games and Mike Shanahan paid the price as head coach of the team in his own Cosmic Cow Pie. You just never know when those pies are going to fly!

In each chapter, there are check marks next to an action you can take, and at the end of each chapter, there is a summary of the Principle discussed in each chapter along with a space to record your notes. After reading the book, decide what you are going to do to connect all the dots in your Cosmic Cow Pie!

Let's get started...Take a look at some the concepts flying around in the Cosmic Cow Pie that need connecting to create balance in our lives. Add more ideas and put them in order of importance to you. Try this as an individual or with your family or a group of friends. Enjoy this "Reality Writing" in the form of Reality Reading!

Some of the Cow Pies of Life Flying Around Us...

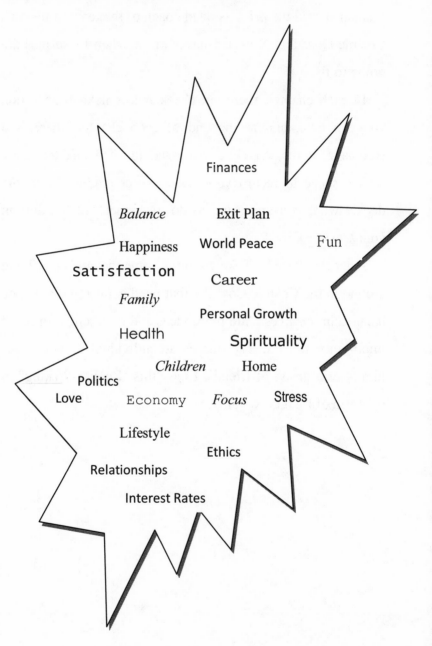

Your Notes

✓ What other Cow Pies are flying around your Universe?

(Go ahead...you can write in the book!)

Chapter One

SWSWSWN

Some Will,
Some Won't,
So What,
Next

One

Some Will, Some Won't, So What, Next
SWSWSWN --- SW3N

Most of our parents taught us to try to please other people, not to make waves and to be respectful and polite in our behavior. Being respectful and polite are qualities we should express. However, we should not constantly worry about the fact someone may not like our ideas, or us, when we FOCUS and know the direction we are taking.

For example, some people may be critical of our behavior if we are self-directed when we stand up for what is right and are not afraid to voice our opinions. The naysayers are often times jealous. They might want to make the thoughtful individual look bad for being creative or taking a risk. The person passing judgment does this because they do not have a strategy or any ideas so they want to tear the self-directed person down.

You should completely understand and be comfortable with the fact not everyone is going to like you or how you think, even though your mother thought so. Be firm in knowing and understanding <u>S</u>ome people <u>W</u>ill like you, <u>S</u>ome people <u>W</u>on't like you, and it really does not matter, so you say <u>S</u>o <u>W</u>hat, <u>N</u>ext. This is the **SWSWSWN** principle or **SW3N**.

Do not take rejection personally. It is just negative energy that you can brush off and kick to the curb. In your personal life or at work, when you understand the **SW3N** principle you will be free from thinking everyone is going to like you. People who participate in recreational drugs might not be individuals you would want to have lunch with or do anything socially. Why would you care if they liked you or not? You shouldn't, so you can certainly understand how not wanting to associate yourself with that behavior allows you to move forward and look for the next friend.

✓ In moments like these, when you begin to feel inadequate or start to question yourself, apply the principles of **SW3N**!

I have a very strong business personality. If someone was involved with me in a transaction and was not doing their part of the deal, I would tell them, directly, what they were doing wrong. If they did not take responsibility after letting them know, I had no problem telling their boss. This behavior did not sit well with many associates and so there were agents who did not like me. I had one experience where I had let an individual know what she needed to do to complete her side of the transaction and she was not happy with me. Thinking she had hung up the phone after speaking with me, she started talking to a friend about me and the phone was still off the receiver. The individual I had just spoken to was describing me as a "female dog" and how I was such a pain in the rear and how she did not like me. The other person in the room said she knew me and said, "Carra does know her business; she is not someone I would want to have lunch with but she gets the job done." Both those people did not care for me but one had respect for how I did my business. Did I care? Not at all, on the personal level. I just wanted to finish the job. I understood the principle of **SW3N**.

Most people know Rhett Butler's final words to the selfish Scarlett O'Hara in **GONE WITH THE WIND**. They were married with a daughter, but the death of their child made Rhett realize that their troubled relationship was beyond salvage. He packed to leave and Scarlett begged him to stay, asking, "Where will I go? What will I do?" Rhett then delivers the immortal line, "Frankly, my dear, I don't give a damn," making it clear the relationship was irrevocably severed.

> *Frankly, my dear, I don't give a damn.*
>
> *- Gone With the Wind*

Rhett moved on to the **NEXT** chapter in his life and told Scarlett just what he thought. Moving on in life from people who do not accept you is the best behavior for your personal growth in connecting all your dots to make you who you are, and free from caring what others think. The next time someone makes you feel bad about something you have done or said, think about **SW3N** and be happy in knowing that you are moving on to the **NEXT** individual who might just care.

Principle Number 1: SWSWSWN

Understand and accept this fact: not everyone is going to like you. Know who you are and always do the right thing. Apply this principle and move on because the **NEXT** person might understand you and could appreciate your position.

Your Notes

Chapter Two

I Get It, I Don't Get It

Understanding this concept will help you have less stress when trying to communicate.

Some people just don't GET IT! Accept this fact!

Two

I Get It, I Don't Get It

Some people just plain "Don't Get It." Learn this principle, accept it, and life will be much easier. You can stay focused on your plan and not discouraged by people who do not accept what you are trying to explain.

✔ You can stay balanced by just understanding that some people, no matter what you say or how you reframe your ideas, Do Not Get It!

To share how I learned this concept, I will describe a two-hour meeting I attended while working with an education advisory group for a local school district administering federal funds for education of the homeless students. A good friend of mine had asked me to represent "business" on a steering committee of volunteers who decided which schools received funds for programs designed to help educate the homeless children.

I was happy to bring my knowledge, talents, and skills to the table to help this worthy cause. The meeting was close to Christmas time and held at a homeless shelter. I was not really thinking when I dressed for the day around the holidays. Just for a little laugh, picture the holiday red Christmas suit I had on with my rhinestone festive pin as I had other places to go after the meeting. When driving to the downtown shelter I realized I should have worn something else, but it was too late and I just had to make the best of it. I felt seriously out of place entering the doors with my red Christmas outfit on, but I could not change the situation. I built a bridge and got over it. I was used to living out of my comfort zone.

At the meeting, one of the applicant schools had not spent the last $3,000 of the previous year's federal funds and wanted to keep it. For me, this was a no brainer. The school made a mistake and they would have to return the funds, as it was a federal program. They had not spent the money during the year so it had to go back. Trying to connect the dots in any other way on a federal program seemed to be a useless waste of time to me.

There were seven Social Service agencies represented at the meeting and discussion started about how the children needed those funds and they could use them for after school programs, snacks, tutors, and school supplies. The conversation continued over an hour and I just sat there listening to the concerns, knowing that everything mentioned was valid. I did not see any way they could keep the funds because of federal funding regulations. Since I had the bright red "main stream" suit on, I thought I should just keep my mouth shut and let them talk. After an additional 30 minutes of the discussion with the group asking my friend, the program director, to call the federal government and ask them if the funds could carry over to the next school year, I could not keep my mouth shut one more minute. I exclaimed, "If you spend the long distance money to call the Federal Government and ask them to extend the time to spend the $3,000, what do you think they will say?" The program director replied, "Sorry, you didn't spend it so the grant money goes back to the fund." The committee was very concerned and still wanted her to call. Since my friend worked for the advisory group, she had to do what the group wanted her to do. When the meeting was over, I asked her why she let it go on so long. She explained the fact the advisory group job description was to make decisions on the funding and she had to listen to what the majority of the group wanted. After all that time the group still thought there was a possibility of getting that $3,000 back to the kids.

This was the moment when I shared with my friend that I was going to design a campaign-type button that said, on the top, **I GET IT** and on the bottom half, **I DON'T GET IT**.

I told her that we could also design T-shirts to sell. It is now almost eighteen years later and the idea has become a reality based on my experience with her group. It appeared to me that it didn't matter what was said to the group, they were not going to accept the fact that if you do not spend federal funds in the year they are allocated, they would go back to the government.

After that meeting, I decided that I would never spend another two hours of my life trying to listen or help people understand concepts they were never going to accept.

I now just see people with the button side up which says **I GET IT** or I see them with the button side up that says **I DON'T GET IT** and move on. Remember the principle of **SWSWSWN!** I learned my lesson and it is easier to understand not all people will **GET IT**. That was the day my dots started connecting.

There are daily opportunities to apply the Cosmic Cow Pie principles. The key to balance is applying what you have learned to the tornado-like events we experience in our lives. Bonnie Raitt wrote a song about the concept of not "Getting It" in love entitled, *I Can't Make You Love Me.* You cannot make someone love you if he or she does not **GET IT**. Read the lyrics Bonnie Raitt wrote and see what you think about processing unreciprocated love. In the big scheme of things, it is easier on you just to forget trying to help someone understand something they do not

Turn down the lights, turn down the bed
Turn down these voices inside my head
Lay down with me, tell me no lies
Just hold me close, don't patronize –
don't patronize me

Cause I can't make you love me if you don't
You can't make your heart feel something it won't

-Bonnie Raitt

want to comprehend. Take deep breaths...picture them with the button and let go. You will laugh inside because you **GET IT** and they do not. Your dots are connecting and theirs are not. You have peace in the Cosmic Cow Pie and they are still out there with their **"I Don't Get It"** button flashing!

You need to know, some people will **NEVER GET IT**. We should have compassion for them in their struggle but move on from your experience and not have a pit in your stomach about that individual and their understanding of the situation.

Principle Number 2: I Get It, I Don't Get It

Understanding this concept will help you have less stress when trying to communicate. Some people just Don't GET IT! Accept this concept! Apply the principle when someone does just not understand you. Forget trying to change their mind and move on.

Your Notes

Chapter Three

Always Have a Plan B

This would infer you have a Plan A in place!

Three

Always Have a Plan B

Having a plan requires preparation, and it pays off. Thirty years ago, a Harvard Study proved that people who wrote down their goals made ten times more money than those who did not have written goals. In the book, **WHAT THEY DON'T TEACH YOU AT HARVARD BUSINESS SCHOOL,** by Mark McCormack, the author describes a study conducted on students in the 1979 Harvard MBA program. In that year, the students responded to the question, "Have you set clear, written goals for your future and made plans to accomplish them?" Only three percent of the graduates had written goals and plans; 13 percent had goals, but they were not in writing; and a whopping 84 percent had no specific goals at all.

> *A brief memory jog about goal setting: You **KNOW** how to do this; you have to be like Nike and Just DO IT!*

Ten years later, the members of the class responded again, and the findings, while somewhat predictable, were nonetheless astonishing. The 13 percent of the class who had goals were earning, on average, twice as much as the 84 percent who had no goals at all. Guess what happened to the three percent who had clear written goals? They were earning, on average, ten times as much as the other 97 percent.

In spite of such proof of success, most people do not have clear, measurable, time-bounded goals. It is not hard to make plans and goals. It just takes some quiet time with yourself to determine what it is you want to do. How hard is that? When we have our lives going crazy in the Cosmic Cow Pie and it seems like we are on autopilot, it is VERY hard. So take some time to STOP and be quiet. The key word is "quiet"; you cannot listen if you are talking. Block out all the external noise that keeps you from hearing new ideas. If you are listening for new ideas to come, you will hear them. Process your values and ponder how the actions in your life reflect the things you value most. What does this mean? Think about what is important to you. Identify HOW you are going to bring the goals into your consciousness and ultimately your life. Once you have Plan A together, you need to have a backup plan or **Plan B** in place.

Start with the BIG picture... where are you going and how do you get there? For example, identify what you want with Career, Finances, Love, Family, Philanthropy, Health, Personal Growth, Education, and your "Exit Plan."

The "Exit Plan" concept, in this context, relates to the bridge we all have to cross when thinking about retirement. The sooner you start to identify how you are going to arrive, the more focused your Cosmic Cow Pie will become. Thinking Social Security is going to get you where you need to be might not be something that is valid at this point in the American economy. Therefore, making plans for a different cash flow later in your life is something you should start thinking about, no matter what your age. With the recent changes in the economy, Plan A might not be valid and **Plan B** is definitely something you will need to investigate.

Start with the big picture of where you want to be in a specific amount of time. This could be a 10-year plan, a 20-year plan, or 30-year plan. It all depends on where you are in life. A friend of mine just started his new 30-year plan on his 70th birthday. He knew what he wanted and where he was going. He felt better because he HAD a plan.

Now break down your plan into achievable segments. What footsteps do you have to take to help go forward with the dream? If you do not write it down and follow a plan, it might not happen. So, start with the simple steps of dreaming about what you want, and then go out to make it happen!

Take, for example, this year: Holidays, Birthdays, Anniversaries, Vacation, Education, Savings, Investments, and Family. Write them all down so you work within the gaps. These are appointments in your life that should not be broken if you want the real balance. Put them in your planner in pen. Make the dates NON-negotiable items. Then work your plan and identify what you need to do each month to meet those responsibilities. Break down the month to each week, and then each day, to achieve this year's goals.

✔ When you get up in the morning, you should have a plan. You will also need a **Plan B** for the day in case it does not go the way you outlined it. If you always have a **Plan B**, you are never devastated if Plan A does not work out. You have prepared yourself for the worst it could be and that way you will always be ready for the asteroids that come from the Cosmic Cow Pie. This is a very important concept to teach children at an early age. It saves many hours of agony when something does not work out.

If you are in need of a goal setting or direction REFRESHER course or a Reinventing Yourself Rehab Opportunity, check out **www.CosmicCowPie.com** for some new ideas.

No matter how carefully you plan a project, something may still go wrong with it. The saying, "the best laid plans of mice and men often go awry" is adapted from an

> *It has been said.... The best laid plans of mice and men often go awry.*

original Irish poem in a line from "To a Mouse," by Robert Burns: "The best laid schemes o' mice an' men gang aft agley." This 18th century poem explores what happens to a mouse when her world turns upside down when a plough disrupts her winter nest and family. Interesting how the "mouse" concept trickled down to the 20th century in **WHO MOVED MY CHEESE** by Spencer Johnson, M.D. He talks about a mouse and the quest for survival in a maze.

Both allegories have the same message. Even if you have a plan, life is going to change so you had better prepare to go in a different direction if something upsets your situation. Today, it is easy to see that we are going to have change. The status quo of the past eight years is coming to a halt. The economic mainstays are tumbling and the government is stepping in to try and help save the day. The handwriting is on the wall. Things as we know them are not going to stay the same, so you better start making a **Plan B** with your life so you won't be steam rolled by the light in the tunnel which IS a freight train coming at you.

If you are in an industry that looks like it could topple, start making **Plan B**. Our economy ran up the heights of the pinnacle. If you take a look at all the goods and services we really do not need, you can catch a glimpse of a possible correction. Keep your eyes open as you walk through any store and look at all the items for sale. Someone had to make those items, someone had to ship them, someone had to stock them, and now someone has to buy them. In the event people stop buying those "non-essential" items, what is going to happen to the business that is trying to sell them? I think you know. Plan A is not working anymore.

My thoughts are simply observations over the past two years. They seem to be indicating at some point the music will stop and there will not be any more chairs. So think about your life, think about how you are going to dig in and ride out the storm because the "perfect storm" could be on its way. This fact is why it is imperative to have a **Plan B**. How will you eat and feed your family? What knowledge, talent and skills do you have to put gas in your car and pay your rent or mortgage if your current employment changes? Families need to discuss this situation together because at some point the government may be out of money.

A short example of having a **Plan B** is a recent trip to the airport. My family was in Las Vegas at the Mandalay Bay Hotel. We had an early morning flight to Hawaii and so spent the night there instead of driving in from Lake Havasu City, Arizona. We needed to leave for the airport at 4:00 a.m. I had called a shuttle service to pick us up and confirmed they would be there at 4:00 a.m. As we went to the pickup area, I felt a possibility that the shuttle might not show up and then what would we do? There was a limo service in the same pick up area and of course, a taxi was always available. When the shuttle did not show up at the pick-up area, I had already spoken to the limo service and they were ready to take us all for $19 to the airport. **Plan B** was in effect and there was no stress, even though the Shuttle service did not arrive. We prepared for a different plan.

When working a business deal, sometimes I will have a **Plan B, C,** and **D**. If one direction does not work, an immediate turn can take place and everyone is prepared to go on the new path. Preparing yourself, customers, or family for the fact that the original plan might not work will help everyone know they do have choices, and **Plan B** can go into effect if needed to accomplish a goal. Another plan is to go forward to the same destination, just in a different way. Can you see how much easier this concept will make your life? If you anticipate the fact that things might not work out the way you wanted them to and you have the confidence to go forward with **Plan B**, you can focus and balance your life. There is less stress in your life when **Plan B** is part of your planning process in everything you do.

Michael Bloomberg, the Mayor of New York City was on "Meet the Press" on September 21, 2008 after AIG was bailed out the first time by the government. He said, about the current economic crisis, "I am planning for the worst and hoping for the best." This man is independently wealthy and works for the City of New York for $1 per year. He understands always having a **Plan B** to succeed.

Principle 3: Always Have a Plan B

If you always have a **Plan B**, you will never experience devastation as you have already reconciled yourself to the fact that your first plan might not work. You will focus and prepare for the obstacles flying around in the Cosmic Cow Pie. Apply this to everything you plan to do.

Your Notes

Chapter Four

You Do Not Need Dr. Phil, Just Pretend!

Four

You Do Not Need Dr. Phil, Just Pretend!

Dr. Phil is a TV icon and gets to the bottom line. He brings out communication in the parties, identifies the REAL problem, and asks, "How's that workin' for you?"

I had explored the concept with my friends, jokingly articulating, "Let's pretend we are on Dr. Phil and see how we would work through this." The principle worked in a practice world with friends and relatives. We would play things out and laugh about how it would be on TV. With specific role playing techniques, we concluded how things in THEORY should be resolved.

A friend and I would walk in the mornings. She was always having men issues so we would play the Dr. Phil game. When she was honest, it worked for her after she applied it. When she was not honest with herself or the person involved it did not work out, as both parties were not in tune with the truth and respect. Honesty has to be part of the Dr. Phil philosophy or it does not work. She was proof dishonesty in any relationship will not work no matter how good a person can lie.

I practiced "Let's pretend we are on Dr. Phil" with another friend about communicating with her mother after her mother moved in with her. My friend was finding her older mother did not really voice what she needed or how she wanted to participate. My husband and I experienced this problem when my mother lived with us. It seemed like my friend was supposed to know what her mother wanted by osmosis, which created a feeling of uncertainty when she was not sure of what the mother wanted, or needed. The Dr. Phil model to resolution might incorporate sitting down with the individual to discuss a specific issue. Many times, it is best if the participants make a list of the things they would like to discuss. The TV show tries to keep everyone being respectful of one another, and has each one who voices a problem also suggest a specific solution. Everyone must be honest, then take responsibility for their actions, and agree to modify behavior. The concept is simple, so practice the principle because it will work.

As the world evolves and many generations are experiencing job or retirement losses, the Dr. Phil theory can work when family members come together. Good communication skills are necessary. Lack of dedication to making the resolution skills work is "PPCS": Poor Personal Communication Skills. This is a problem many people experience and have a hard time overcoming.

I learned "PPCS" from my mother in 1990 while living in Maui, Hawaii. She had come with us to Maui from Colorado in 1988 after having been divorced for twenty years. I was an only child, so when we were moving to Maui we asked if she would like to come with us. It was a nice addition as we had our four-year-old daughter and eighteen-year-old stepdaughter moving to Maui. We brought our own support group to the Island. Our family had a comfortable home backing to Haleakala ranch in Kula. The property had an ohana, which is a living unit attached to the house. It was really my mother's own small home behind our oversized garage. It connected to the house through a roofline that covered a deck between both dwellings.

We learned a lot about each other and sometimes not the easy way. Had we known about the Dr. Phil principle and how to work through things, we might have had better hearing, as the decibel of some of our conversations probably did damage the eardrums. We really did not work well through family issues at certain times.

One afternoon my mother asked my husband and me to come over to her ohana. We arrived not knowing what would come of this invitation. She sat in the cane chair across from us and in a very loud voice shouted, "PPCS."

> *When the student is ready, the master appears.*
>
> *-Buddhist Proverb*

Then she repeated it again. We just looked at each other not wanting to laugh but neither of us had a clue of what "PPCS" meant. She laughed with an arrogant look on her face and said "poor personal communication skills." Then we did laugh and she became furious. As we sat together, we did resolve some issues the way Dr. Phil would. The "PPCS" event opened up the communication process and we all talked about things that were bothering us living in our current situation. The lesson was important in communication to be able to talk about anything. Even more important was the voice or attitude with which we had the conversation. The old adage of "it's not what you say but how you say it" became clear.

Personal pride sometimes takes over in conflict and instead of thinking about how a problem can be resolved, people think about how it makes them look if they did something wrong. Most individuals do not like failure or want to appear as if they made a mistake. Since the feeling of failure is something most people find hard to deal with, they will avoid talking about something all together. All I can say to this behavior is to get over it and think about always doing the right thing.

✓ Learn to communicate honestly and you will experience much less stress along with more balance. Dr. Phil shares similar concepts in almost every TV episode.

I was ready to apply the Dr. Phil concept of honest communication in the Cosmic Cow Pie, so the opportunities appeared. I am not a PHD in psychology, or Masters Candidate in counseling. I was a sales person for 30 years who learned everyone makes decisions differently and processes information in their own

> *When the student is ready, the lesson appears.*
>
> *-Gene Oliver*

unique style. I took many classes on personality types and I thought I knew how to work with everyone. However, I found different obstacles as I began a new chapter in life, trying to live balance in retirement. What planet did I come from thinking that retirement offered new horizons of utopia and I had arrived at the destination ready for paradise? Retirement was not the utopia I had envisioned during my hectic work years.

I started volunteering at a local food bank and really had the feeling I could make a difference and at the same time was make people laugh. Living love could only describe what I felt after I had been working at the food bank for a week, and I was excited about the response we had from the diners. I could see lots of potential for things we would do to help those in need. Then one day, a conflict arose between the food bank director and me, in front of a group of other volunteers. It felt like someone had physically hit me with a 2 x 4 in the head and came in the form of a 16-tissue shock as my composure crumbled. My vision of celestial bliss came to an implosion that day, as I was wallowing in the success of the past week of giving back to humanity. All of a sudden, a Cosmic Cow Pie was enveloping me.

One day, before a scheduled meeting, the manager of the food bank told me my excitement over helping and offering suggestions was a threat or a criticism to what he was doing. He told me as a volunteer I should not come in telling him what to do. He told me this before a volunteer meeting which was devastating to me as I was just thinking about how much good could be done to help his diners. I had let all the walls down from my sales life. I thought working with people who woke up every morning and did things to help the world be a better place would be different. In my distorted picture of the life of a volunteer, everything would be joyful, respectful, and full of feelings of kindness.

My fairy tale idea of being a volunteer to make a difference in the world came to an immediate halt at the food bank that day. I agonized about how attacked I felt and how my idealistic concept of life in helping others was not as I pictured. The thoughts swallowing my consciousness were feelings of hurt, humiliation, and disappointment in the American ideal. The guilt I had felt in not going into social work or doing something to help the world in a humanitarian way as a career was over. I was an educated individual who could get things done and the center manager could not see that or even give me a chance. The disappointment was overwhelming and as the meeting started, I did not know if I could compose myself and participate. When the chair asked me to report on my activities of the past evening, I could not talk and burst out in tears. I said I needed to speak later in the meeting after I could get myself together. I just tried to cry quietly. Then they came back to me and I decided I had nothing to lose. I had already cried in a business meeting and at this point, I did not really care what others thought of me. The wall went back up and the **SW3N** principle took over.

I suggested we **"pretend we are on Dr. Phil"** as I thought there had been a misunderstanding. We needed some honest communication because this situation just "wasn't working for us." The food bank director said he was going to quit the group and let his assistant take his place, as they did not need two people from their office at the meeting. I pleaded with him not to quit and that as a new volunteer I was over zealous in sharing my ideas. The things I had expressed were not a criticism of what he was doing and that I was sincerely sorry if I had offended him. I explained to him that I was the one that needed to resign from the group so he could stay and implored him not to leave; it was my mistake in being so excited to help. I described how I wanted to help the world and how I had always felt guilty in not doing something that was more service oriented, like being a teacher or working as a social service provider. I was now in a position to be a volunteer and I had just messed everything up and again begged with him to accept my apology and stay with the project. I chirped all this out to the entire group with tears streaming down my face. I could not believe this was happening. How naive I was in the ways of the world. As I finished my plea, the director said he would stay with the group and the meeting continued.

Later in the meeting, the director of the food bank asked to speak with me outside and we had a wonderful talk. He explained that he was under criticism for some of the things he does because he does not have an exuberant personality. Actually, he was an engineer with little or no emotion so when I came in all excited about what we had accomplished the night before and had some ideas that might make the program even better, he felt threatened again, about how he runs the food bank. He said he was dealing with a sense of remorse for changing to the food bank job, as he quit employment where he made twice as much, to help humanity. The diners at the food bank did not appreciate him and the volunteers were always telling him how to do his job. He too had the vision of helping people and it did not turn out to be what he thought. We ended with hugs and respect. We went back into the meeting and it was very productive.

The director and I explained our feelings, described the misunderstanding, and shared how we came to a meeting of the minds. We had worked through things by **"pretending**

we were on Dr. Phil." When it was time to adjourn I asked if anyone would comment to me about what had happened in the meeting as everyone did hear the discussion, the threat of leaving and the resolution after pretending we were on Dr. Phil. One member of the committee in her late fifties expressed to the group "it was a life changing event." She said she had never seen such conflict resolution in action and so quick. She thanked me for my tears and knew she would be different because of the experience.

To practice the Dr. Phil concept, I would like to encourage a 21st century idea for those looking to find balance as life changes in front of our eyes. To practice this principle, try a social networking space on facebook, as an individual, a group, a couple, or any combination, to discuss the individual chapters and experiences applying the principles of the concepts in Cosmic Cow Pie. Go to www.CosmicCowPie.com to connect to a group of cyber readers and join the discussions. In Hawaii, when a huge wave was coming, surfers would say, "Eddy would go" so you can go to cyber space to chat like Eddy Aikau, the world famous surfer. Share how you might be connecting the dots with the chapters in this book, or just make your own notes after each chapter.

Principle 4: You Do Not Need Dr. Phil,

Just Pretend!

If you are in a situation when there is conflict, apply this principle and think about how Dr. Phil would work out the problem. Dr. Phil would ask, "How's that workin' for you"? He would encourage honesty and respect of the parties to a come to a mutual resolution.

Your Notes

Chapter Five

Build a Bridge And Get Over It

If you can't change the outcome of a circumstance, process it and MOVE ON!

Five

Build a Bridge and Get Over It

Life is full of experiences that are painful or embarrassing and moving on from the uncomfortable feeling is an exhilarating accomplishment. A simple way to execute this concept is to **Build a Bridge and Get Over It**. Many motivational speakers have promoted the bridge principle and when it becomes a habit in your life, you will feel free and balanced.

✓ There are two simple questions to ask yourself to determine if you are going to walk over the bridge and leave your baggage behind. Is there anything I can do to change this circumstance? Do I want to change it? If you are really done with the situation and ready to move on, put on your walking shoes and go for the other side of the bridge.

Getting to the place in your mind to let go and walk over the bridge can be a challenge. In my own experience, I had a colossal problem letting go of anger. At age sixteen, my parents got a divorce. In 1969, divorce was not common in the community where I grew up. I had only one friend who was from a divorced family and she seemed "different" because she did not have a father at home. The divorce blind-sided me, as my parents did not argue in front of me. They had matching motorcycles, snowmobiles, and matching striped pant outfits. To society and me, it appeared as though we were the "Leave It to Beaver" family. I was clueless to the fact I could suddenly become a victim of divorce.

> *The Serenity Prayer*
> God grant me the serenity to accept the things I cannot change; courage to change the things I can; and wisdom to know the difference.
>
> *-Reinhold Niebuhr*

I did not feel like I was a victim at the time; I was just angry. My mother had been devastated and it was hard to help her be happy. I decided to graduate from high school a year early and get on with my life. I went to a trade school in New York City called the French Fashion Academy at 555

Madison Avenue. Coming from a small town in Colorado, New York City was a long way from home. One day my dad called and vented, "There is no more money for you to stay at the school and you need to come home." I exclaimed that I would figure it out, pay for myself, and stay to finish the year. The lessons I learned in New York City were instructions I took with me through life and made me who I am today. I figured out how to work and survive to stay at school. I built a bridge and walked to the other side where independence reigned.

It was not until many years later I was able to build a bridge for a relationship with my dad and move on. Today we have a relatively normal rapport and I am no longer angry. The bridge did take a long time to build but nonetheless, I did build it.

As I move through life, I find many times when there is nothing I can do about a situation and once I let it go and move on, it creates less stress and I am ready for the next event that will inevitably come down the road. In my business life, there were always things that did not work out the way I had hoped. I learned quickly to **Build the Bridge and Get Over It**, not looking back.

I practiced this principle so well that I wc things in a nanosecond. A few years ago, m pointed out to me how fast I got over things. Whi.. un a trip to London, I received a call from her distraught and in tears. She had just broken up with her first serious boyfriend from college. I assured her that life would go on. I explained that she had shared some wonderful learning experiences with him and she would always have those memories. It was not a comfort but she tried to accept the reassurance. She told me she needed more than my three seconds of sadness to be over it. We both laughed but her comments did put into perspective how rapidly I moved over bridges.

> *I just want to be mad for a while*
> *I think I'm right I think you're wrong*
> *I'll probably give in before long Please don't make me smile*
> *I just want to be mad for a while.*
>
> *-Teri Clark*

Our family has a fun way of communicating when we are done with a particular subject. We use a hand gesture making an arch indicating to the other person they should build a bridge and get over it. A wonderful way to work on building a bridge is to give yourself some time, and then get over it.

This concept is summed up in a country song written by Teri Clark entitled, *I Just Want to be Mad for a While.*

Many situations in a work environment come up which need bridges, too. Disappointment comes from many avenues. Being prepared to move on in business also insulates you from anger and hurt. In a work environment, it is always good to prepare yourself for the worst it could be, so if things turn out better you are not devastated. I had a call in the office from a man who lived on a street where I had sold several of his neighbor's homes. He wanted to look at a property I had listed to see if it would work for his family of seven. Based on my work ethic, when a buyer called and only wanted to look at one house, I would be prepared to show several more in case they did not like the one where we had an appointment, always have a **Plan B**. In this case, they did not like the house they had called on and I was ready to show them others, **Plan B** was in effect. We looked at the others and they liked one and wanted to pursue a contract. The buyers needed to sell their home before they could purchase another home. I did a market analysis and found that even before going back to their house for a listing appointment, they did not have enough equity to purchase the new home. I did not want to tell them over the phone so I kept the appointment to let them know the sad news. I was thinking I was wasting my time and I had built a bridge and was over it. However, I felt I needed to do the right thing by going to their home to explain it personally. The funny part was they had forgotten I was coming and it was dinnertime with five kids so you know what the atmosphere in the house was like. I told them the news and then like a good salesperson, I asked them if they knew someone else who might want to buy or sell real estate. The wife jumped up and indicated the neighbors across the street were looking for a new Realtor and she dialed their phone number before I could even say a word. She explained what happened and handed me the phone. The neighbor wanted me to come across the street and tell them about the market and warned me that I would only have five minutes to sell myself as her husband was going to go bowling. I ran over, did my presentation, and the husband said, "I never thought you could sell me in five minutes but you have done your homework and I think you can sell my house so I will sign and my wife can finish the rest of the paperwork, while I go to bowl." The neighbor who did not have enough equity did call me the next year as the market changed and they had an increase in income so they listed and sold their home too. By being prepared to cross the bridge and move on, there were successful conclusions for all.

Once you have **Crossed the Bridge**, you might want to set fire to the bridge so you never go back over it again. Leave it behind and if you need a little more symbolism, just see yourself throwing the bad feelings in the river as you cross over. Visualize the problem going downstream and out of your thoughts. This is one of the ways to navigate through the Cosmic Cow Pie and find balance.

Principle Number 5: Build a Bridge

And Get Over It

Apply this principle to your situations. If you cannot change the outcome of a circumstance, process it as such, build a bridge, and walk on over it. Get to the other side and move on, letting your problems go down the river without you.

Your Notes

Chapter Six

Read, Think, And Reason

Six

Read, Think, and Reason

The basic skills we learn in school are reading, writing, and arithmetic. With those skills, we should be able to fill out job applications, communicate, and do math with money for survival. If all human beings had those basic skills, we would be advancing as a world of individuals all being able to understand and communicate with one another.

✓ What we need to add to those skills are thinking and reasoning. For a well-rounded personality, we should be able to **Read, Think, and Reason.**

A friend of mine was the Director for an alternative education class for unwed mothers called OYP, Opportunity for Young Parents. She asked me to be on the Advisory Committee to help these young people prepare to enter society with some survival skills. The program offered videotaped practice interviews, goal setting, and how to survive as single parents. We helped them with balancing checkbooks and **Reasoning** how they were going to get through high school with a child, and several of the young parents had more than one child.

The good news is, most of the students did go out in the world and become productive adults. They were able to take care of themselves and their children. One of the OYP students had five kids before she was 21 and secured a management job, married a young man with a good career, and ended up buying and selling three properties from me as a Real Estate agent and an OYP mentor.

I am sad to say that not all the high school students had these successes when they graduated but the OYP students knew how to **Read, Think, and Reason** as they left to go out in the world on their own.

As a member of the Advisory Committee for our local high school and the OYP program, I had the opportunity to meet with other school districts and network with administrators about what we were learning from our mentor experiences. My feeling was very strong in having classes or even one hour of the day to work with students on how to process information, weigh out the ramifications and then relate what they thought into real life. **Read, Think, and**

Reason were the skills I felt all students needed to have upon graduation.

My idealistic and simplistic input did not go far with the school system but we did implement this concept in our work environment helping every person who worked for us to

> *Knowledge is Power*
>
> *-Sir Francis Bacon 1597*

incorporate these skills into their work ethics. Our daughter learned these skills from early childhood and they are now second nature to her in handling any crises or just life situations that come up daily.

When our youngest daughter was in 1st grade, we would go to the library in Makawao, Maui, Hawaii every week. We were checking out a book and the sign on the librarian's desk said, "Have your book open with your library card ready to be stamped." Our daughter had read the sign, had her book open and card out. The librarian whispered to her, "How did you know to have this all ready?" Our daughter looked at her in disbelief and replied, "I read the sign." We had taught her to be aware of what signs said in every store, what the road signs indicated, and when she was ten, we even had her read the signs in the airport to find the gate for the planes we were to fly on. By the time she went to Spain with her exchange group at 15, as a sophomore, she was an experienced airport navigator with no fear of traveling.

Our daughter's elementary school experience in Kula, Hawaii with the Japanese influence was incredible. We had homework with her to read for 30 minutes a day in kindergarten and we had to initial a reading record proving that we did the reading with her. Wonderful discipline skills developed for her from the very beginning of her school experience. By learning to do her homework when she first got home, she always kept up her grades during her undergraduate and college time. This is a simple concept that you can do with your own children. It might be wise to take up reading 30 minutes a day yourself, for your own personal growth. Take some time to define yourself and calmly process the world events going on around you. The more you know the better you feel about everything. Knowledge is power.

The schools cannot be the only place our children are learning. As explained in my Opportunity for Young Parents experience, the education administration cannot focus on how to **Think and Reason**; they have many other priorities to meet. Parents have to take responsibility to help each child develop this skill at all ages. It takes time and energy to instill this in a child but it is of utmost importance for them to be able to think outside of the box. They need to learn that ANYTHING is possible if you can **Read, Think, and Reason**.

The business community has a responsibility for providing the best service possible as the fight for repeat business is up for grabs in the changing economy. Every employee should be able to **Read, Think, and Reason**. We have individuals who have not learned the skills of thinking and reasoning things out which is why the customer satisfaction in some areas is low. We have become accustomed to accepting mediocre work, disillusioned by the service we receive in many industries.

This should be a wakeup call to businesses all over the world. We need to set a bar of expectation for "A" quality work. We want the "platinum level" of service if we are going to spend our discretionary dollars with a specific business. The service should exceed our expectations so we share our jubilation with the service and we send everyone to that store or company. We will tweet to our friends because we are delighted about how we felt about spending our money there. Business owners should embrace the concept of **Read, Think, and Reason** and help employees understand the concept and process information from a position of power.

Happy past clients are the key to creating an "epidemic" of referral business. Malcolm Gladwell, author of THE TIPPING POINT, goes into detail of how to create an epidemic in any business. Advertising dollars to broadcast a product or service pale in comparison to the most economical form of advertising: word of mouth from a satisfied customer. I hope you **"Get It"** and the concept of **Read, Think, and Reason** will become part of your mantra.

As our economy changes and retail establishments along with businesses of all types are struggling to survive, they need to be sensitive about how every employee interacts with the public. They need to be able to **Read, Think, and Reason**. They need to play out the conversation and make decisions on how their experience would be if the roles were reversed. They need to have some understanding of how their behavior can affect the very survival of the business. They also need to understand there are probably ten individuals, ultimately more qualified to do the same job, waiting for an opportunity for the opening if management is looking for a replacement. If it takes fear as a motivator to modify behavior, any business could consider this concept as they work with their employees in setting a new bar of service expectations. Mediocre service is no longer acceptable. The message is loud and clear that service and exceeding customer expectations is the key to survival in all business in the 21st century.

Take the time to **Read** any information given to you in any situation, then **Think** about what it says and **Reason** how all actions should reflect intelligent processing of the data. Slow down and get off the hamster wheel, take time to reflect instead of react. Do not be afraid to see the truth. To **Think** and **Reason**, you should know when to say "No." This can mean, "No, I can't process this information right now. You will have to wait until I can **Think** about it in a calm manner and **Reason** correctly." Then you will have the right answer. The concept of **Read, Think, and Reason** can save you from costly business and personal mistakes when applied in a sincere, professional manner.

Principle 6: Read, Think, and Reason

The concept of Read, Think, and Reason applies to everything you do. Use your cogitative skills to reason through things. Read all the information you can about a situation, process it by thinking it over, and then reason out the best way to proceed. Being able to Reason out any situation will help you connect the dots in the Cosmic Cow Pie of life and stay balanced.

Your Notes

Chapter Seven

Kicked to the Curb

It just happens!
Be prepared and know when
it is happening to you.
Know when to do it yourself!

Seven

Kicked to the Curb

Life is a big highway with lots of twists and learning curves, and knowing when you have been kicked to the curb or need to kick someone to the curb is one key to finding balance in the Cosmic Cow Pie.

✔ There really are people in the world that do not need to be in your life, and some people probably feel the same about you.

> *Life is a highway, I wanna ride it All night long If you're going my way, I wanna drive it All night long.*
>
> *-Rascal Flatts*
> *-Tom Cochrane*
> *1991*

Sometimes we are the kick"ee" and sometimes we are the kick"or." The kick"ee" receives the kick and the kick"or" gives the kick. Sometimes we are the bat and sometimes the ball. Worst-case scenario, we are the bug on the outside of the windshield.

A person may befriend you to use you and then move on or **Kick you to the Curb** with no remorse. Individuals with another agenda are like wolves in sheep's clothing, lurking around out there in the Cosmic Cow Pie, just looking to latch on to an unsuspecting individual for a free ride. These wolves act like academy award winning actors and can fool even the most discerning personalities. Their goal in life is to suck all the blood out of anyone willing to give them help in the name of good. They will take everything you have to give and then want more while criticizing you to others. Individuals like this are people you need to purge from your life or simply stated, **Kick them to the Curb**.

How do you kick someone to the curb without being too offensive? In a social relationship, the nicest way to do it is to stop communicating and they will get the message loud and clear. If the person is hurt and wants to know why you are not returning calls or e-mails, they will keep contacting you until they are successful. At that point, you need to have a loving way to explain your differences. Today with facebook and Twitter, you can just take them off your friend list or stop following them and that really says it all. You virtually **Kicked them to the Curb**.

Facebook is an exciting tool in social networking and can really make you feel bad or on top of the world as friends sign up to see your life in cyberspace. The main page of the facebook shows how many friends you have with an actual number displayed. Not having any friends on my page was my greatest fear when I first started to participate. I know you read the **SW3N** chapter and are laughing at this statement but it is true. I did not want to look like a friendless person in cyberspace. To avoid rejection anxiety before I registered, I called a few friends I knew on facebook and begged them to accept me as a friend so I would not show up as a loser. The site actually displays when starting up, (name) has no friends. As this networking technique continues and grows to the next level, it has the potential to harm people as individuals take names off their facebook as friends. They are literally **Kicked to the Curb** and the world sees it. A word to the wise is to be careful with what you post or delete on facebook.

I have identified who I want to surround myself with and spend time with, and know my priorities. Some individuals have a negative influence on my life and it is better not to associate with them. One person in particular I was actually trying to help and befriend had a bad reputation around town with drinking and abusive behavior. She had several DUIs and could not drink responsibly. She never drank around me, as she knew how I felt about that behavior. I continually had to defend my position in being her friend with others because of her past actions. The association continued and I found she not only had a drinking problem she also had a bi-polar disorder and on top of that had a hard time with the truth. A mutual friend told me "when her mouth was open she was lying." Because of the personality disorder, she would continually **Kick me to the Curb** and then come back into my life. I believe in turning the other cheek when someone has made a mistake but this woman really needed help and my friendship was not helping her situation. My accepting her invitation back from the curb was really enabling her bad behavior and my kindness was not helping her in any way. It is my understanding she may be getting help now but until she can demonstrate a genuine friendship through her recovery process, it is best I stay at the curb and out of her life.

As you ponder the concept of **Kicked to the Curb**, you will soon start to realize whom you might have done this to and then again who might have done it to you. Get comfortable with the concept as it happens all through your life. As people age, I have found they do not have as much tolerance for the actions of others so kicking friends to the curb does not seem to bother them. This principle goes hand in hand with **SW3N**. As you mature interests change, income levels change, hobbies change, families change, so friends you had earlier in life may not be individuals you want to socialize with later.

Identifying your priorities and the people you want to associate with will help you connect the dots in the Cosmic Cow Pie.

Principle 7: Kicked to the Curb

Whether you are the kick"ee" or the kick"or," get comfortable with the fact not everyone will have a place in your life. Determine those you have a common bond with and make those individuals your extended family.

Your Notes

Chapter Eight

Living Out Of Your Comfort Zone!

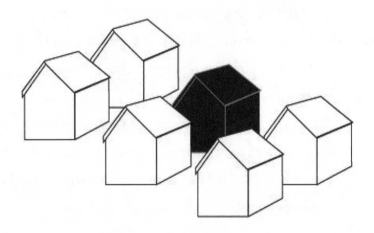

Eight

Living Out Of Your Comfort Zone!

Living out of your comfort zone means doing things you do not want to do. Any type of sales person lives in this atmosphere. After thirty years in sales, this feeling is very natural to me. I get up in the morning and force myself to do all the uncomfortable tasks first. I make myself do things normal people just say "no" to. I push myself too far sometimes thinking that I need to live out of my comfort zone so I can get everything done that needs to be done.

It is my observation that people who live out of their comfort zone actually achieve more.

✓ When you live out of the zone, you push yourself and end up with a greater sense of accomplishment, enjoying what you do as the uncomfortable feeling becomes normal.

Simply talking with someone about an unpleasant subject or speaking in front of a group is another uncomfortable zone for many people. For some, activities that create stress push us to the outer limits of the zone. Some of those things are good for us. By facing the anxiety or fear head on, we become better people.

When I moved to Arizona, I worked in a new community about an hour drive from my home. I thought I needed to make some friends in the area. I was selling homes there and needed to set up a "real time" social network to help baby boomers thinking of retirement connect to a few people. Making new friends in my fifties was way out of my comfort zone. However, I knew I needed to do it. This small community by the Colorado River was not a metropolis, thriving with diversity. I looked everywhere I went to see if there were people I would want to hang out with and have lunch. The prospects are tough for finding friends when you do not have children on the playground or kids in sports. As my daughter grew up, I was always meeting other mothers and dads at school events, so creating a social life with friends was not difficult at all. Now, I was on my own in a new area. Being the over achiever I was, I thought I could meet new friends. I had spent my career going up to people and asking them if they wanted to buy or sell something so I would just change hats and see if they wanted to hang out and have fun. This concept may seem foreign to some but the results of getting out of my comfort zone with a creative idea to make friends has helped many couples enjoy their new surroundings in the next chapter of their lives.

You can't always get what you want No, you can't always get what you want But if you try sometime You just might get what you need

-Rolling Stones

My friend-finding project evolved in the following manner. I decided to create a lunch club. When I met women I thought might be fun to have lunch with, I would just ask them if they wanted to be in my club. I knew I wanted to share with other women of about the same age and socio economic background. I played it out in my mind so if they answered "no" or gave me an excuse as to why they did not want to be in my club, I had already prepared myself for the rejection. Having already embraced the concept of **SW3N**, it felt as if I had nothing to lose by asking and everything to gain by inviting them to lunch. I had one friend who already lived in a new neighborhood I had been selling to some people getting ready to retire so I had the first friend for the lunch club. I met another woman who worked onsite for a builder and who was articulate and professional in how she handled herself at work. She was the first person I did not know well and invited her to the lunch club. She was elated, as she did not know anyone to have fun with in the area because she was relatively new also. The next woman I invited was a neighbor in the housing area who was friends with another Real Estate friend of mine. We started the group with four women and tried adding a few more each time we had lunch, and our group started to grow.

The group evolved into a dinner club where we brought our husbands and had a potluck buffet. This get-together led to a Super Bowl Party where twelve couples came and it was the start of an annual chili cook off. Just for the record, I was the first winner of the event. We lived an hour away so my first friend took over being the director for the group and started organizing Friday Afternoon Club where everyone brought appetizers to someone's house and they had happy hour until midnight. The group grew and people we did not know wanted to be included in the social events. A weekly e-mail is now going out to over sixty couples and there are different events for three to four days out of the week. The activities include stained glass classes, ATV rides in the desert, boating in the summer, Wii bowling competitions, golf outings, morning walks, rafting trips down the Colorado, vodka-tasting parties, and the list goes on.

My husband has his own "lunch bunch" of golfing friends. The guys had the rabbit time, or the first tee time every morning. He did not know a soul when he started playing golf at the club but he introduced himself and his group grew to about six or eight guys who would meet in the mornings to tee off and enjoy breakfast after the round. It also evolved into a social activity with the wives, so more new friendships formed by reaching out.

Getting Out of my Comfort Zone to meet people and help friends make new friends made the retirement chapter forat least fifty couples little bit nicer. Making new friends is always a challenge and some areas, as seen on Sixty Minutes, are now having front porch parties to meet the neighbors and socialize in person. In creating balance in your life, it is important to have all the dots connected including social activities. Rest assured most people are not going to ask you if you want to be in a club, so you can take this idea and make it your own, living out of your comfort zone.

Principle 8: Living Out Of Your Comfort Zone!

Learning how to power through uncomfortable situations by living out of your comfort zone will help you get to an expected end.

Your Notes

Chapter Nine

The Drama Hook

Nine

The Drama Hook

The **Drama Hook** is an overreaction, which catches you and takes you on an exciting ride in life. Adrenaline is the ultimate drama hook and it catches many an unsuspecting soul.

It is a chemical, which sometimes creates a sensation so thrilling you want to keep going back for more. Many of us live on it as stress in our lives creates the rush and keeps supplying our addiction to a natural drug. Adrenaline is a hormone produced by the body when you are frightened, angry or excited, which makes the heart beat faster and prepares the body to fight or flee.

> *Adrenaline*
>
> **Noun:** *a catecholamine secreted by the adrenal medulla in response to stress; stimulates autonomic nerve action Autonomic is produced by internal forces or causes; spontaneous.*

By definition, adrenaline is a spontaneous response to changes in our situations. Many times opportunities arise to feed the need for the rush created by adrenaline. Like the feeling you get when doing something special for the very first time. Or going on vacation to a tropical location, riding in a limousine, receiving beautiful jewelry, getting a promotion, securing a deal you have been working on for a long time, sky diving, bungee jumping, race car driving or scuba diving. Your sensory perceptions heighten by the occurrence of certain events called **Drama Hooks**.

It is important to know the emotions you might be feeling could all be associated with the natural adrenaline you get when addicted to **Drama Hooks**. The response actions you take under the influence of the **Drama Hook** can be fatal to relationships and your financial status.

✓ It is important to keep the **Drama Hooks** in check and take time to determine if you are being caught by a drama hook or listening to a door which is opening for a new possibility to the benefit of you and your family.

The emotional roller coaster of the adrenaline in your system needs controlling. Using the principles in the Cosmic

Cow Pie will help in relieving stress and getting to that place of balance in your life.

People become adrenaline junkies looking for the next rush. They become addicted to the excitement and danger that invariably becomes involved. Most people do not realize what is actually happening in their bodies. They become confused with the feelings and sensations. Sometimes the mechanisms of adrenaline respond to avoid pain and are beneficial in survival. Other times adrenaline can make one feel detached from reality and alienated from friends and relatives.

I am a drama queen. I have a tendency to take the bait on many ideas. After 34 years of marriage, my husband can deal with the ups and downs of someone always looking for a new idea to investigate and helps me learn to determine if the concept is valid or another **Drama Hook**.

In 1983, the Drama Hook caught me when we decided to purchase a $60,000 three-axis engraving machine that would engrave on brass, acrylic or wood. The reason I became a Real Estate agent in 1979 was to save enough money to open our own retail store. The real estate market was good to us and we saved the money to start a business. We thought we could hire people to run the store, manage it from behind the scenes, and still have real estate sales income. I thought if one store was good, then two stores would be better. Despite my husband's best efforts to dissuade me from going forward with the purchase of the second machine; he acquiesced to my **Drama Hook** rush. We completed the purchase of the two machines. We had a store in Estes Park, Colorado called Colorado's Incredible Machine and a second store in Lake Tahoe, California called Tahoe's Incredible Machine. I am sure you have figured out the rest of the story. We did not make money since we were not participating on a daily basis. The financial loss to my **Drama Hook** was over $500,000.

We have recovered and licked those wounds from that adventure and I have learned my lesson about the **Drama Hook** principle. I now openly question my ideas to discern if they are **Drama Hooks** or something I should be doing. I speak from experience on every chapter in this book and hope in some small way I can make a difference and save you from some of the expensive and painful lessons I have learned.

Every age group has the potential for the **Drama Hook** rush. I knew a young man who needed help getting started on a career as he took a break from college. He needed to earn enough money to go back to school. I helped him from the beginning of his career to see him become the top salesperson for a new homebuilder in an Arizona community by the Colorado River. He came to me one day after shopping the competition for the builder he worked with and told me he could get in line to purchase a new home for only $500 down and the sales price was very reasonable at $109,000. The way the market had been increasing it appeared he could sell the finished home and make a quick $40,000. He wrote the contract and he did make the money. He then went up in price to purchase another home at $350,000 and expected to make $100,000 when he sold it. He took out a second mortgage on the new home for $100,000 to use to leverage in and purchase more real estate. About this time, he called and asked me what I thought. He was going to buy a lot and build a half a million dollar house and expected to make another half million on the turn. I told him specifically that this was a **Drama Hook** and he needed to stop. He did not listen and went ahead to buy the lot. He also asked me about another condominium he wanted to buy and again, I told him I liked the location of the project but I did not know how many pieces of property he could support. He had already purchased another lot in the desert so was now land poor and in debt to the max. He lost his job and got behind in the payments on all his real estate. He lost the house to foreclosure and both lots. He had to move back home and start over after making more than $200,000 in commissions as a young man of twenty-four years old. He now knows what a **Drama Hook** is and will not make the same mistake again.

Principle 9: The Drama Hook

To maintain inner peace and balance, do not take the bait on the Drama Hook. If you keep yourself focused, you will be able to connect all the dots in the Cosmic Cow Pie and know the difference between an idea to pursue and a Drama Hook.

Your Notes

Chapter Ten

Just Step Over It...
The Bar of Expectations

Ten

Just Step Over It... The Bar of Expectations

Just Step Over It is a principle that lowers stress in today's world of mediocre service. This does not help the world become a better place but it can help you process your experience with less anxiety. Learning how to deal with the current service industry will allow you to keep focused on your task and not get distracted when others do not perform at a level you expect.

✓ Lowering your expectation prevents anger and will aid in processing obstacles in the Cosmic Cow Pie.

This concept is a challenge to all industry to look and listen to what customers are experiencing in today's world. If you are a business owner, "inspecting what

> *"Inspect what you expect."*
>
> *-Zig Ziglar seminar, 1981*

you expect" in service would be one way of knowing what your customers are receiving and keeping your bar higher.

My personal bar of expectations started as I was growing up in a home where my mother and dad had gone to college in the early 1950's. Work of average quality was not acceptable for me according to their rules. My mother was a teacher and my dad worked for a major auto company in corporate sales. The expectations for my schoolwork were for A's; however, some B's passed without comment. In other areas of my life, if I started an activity at the beginning of the year, I had to follow through until the end of the year. I was not to be a quitter and I was supposed to do my best work possible in all of my activities.

I strived to a high level of achievement and my expectations were that others shared those same goals and aspirations. I worked and socialized with people who did exhibit those qualities. I selected vendors in my field of work who also valued a high standard of service.

My observation of service today is a visual of a high jump bar. The top of the bar would represent "A" quality work but because of the mediocrity of today's workers, we have to set that bar down to the middle where average work is acceptable. When the restaurant server forgets to fill your coffee after you have asked twice you can see that bar drop down to the "D" or "D minus" category. If she forgets it all together after the third request, you can see the bar on the ground, and if you have to ask another server to help, you have learned to just **step over it**. Another example of poor service told by one of my clients was that he needed a Geiger Counter just to find the bar under the ground since there had been so many mistakes on his documentation for a closing with a bank.

It could be I am getting older and noticing a difference in the quality of work ethics but there appears to be a change in the air. As I wander around in the Cosmic Cow Pie, I seem to be more and more irritated by the mediocrity that seems to be running rampant. However, being angry at poor quality of service creates stress and keeps me from connecting all the dots to achieve balance. I recently read a blog on mediocrity where the writer said we must be the example in our behavior and that will show others the way. I am not sure how to change the attitude of the entry-level service providers but until the quality of work changes or employers expect a higher standard of performance it seems we must lower the bar of expectations and just **step over it**.

Try not to be angry with the computer help who barely speaks English or the receptionist who does not even know the mailing address of the company and directions to the business from any major landmark. I can speak with the employees and now just chuckle and **step over the bar** instead of being upset. Recently, I called the county to obtain a form for a tax appeal. In my world, if I were sending out the notifications of how to appeal a tax assessment, I would have the web site information printed on the paper for the appeal. If the county included the website information to obtain the forms, there would be fewer phone calls, and they would have saved time and productivity of employees. This example of mediocrity does not stop there. The phone number the county sent out did not have the direct line to the assessor's office. Therefore, someone from the county had to answer the phone, listen to the caller to identify what the caller needed, and then transfer the call to someone in the assessor's office. When I got to the assessor's office, the individual answering the phone did not have the web site handy to let me know where to look online and even further stupidity was demonstrated when he did not know the time frame the sold comparables needed to be taken from to protest the taxes. I had to **step over the bar** as my expectation for quality service had disappeared.

Complaining about service in America is not going to change unless companies are aware of what the customers are feeling about substandard work ethics and they do something about it. I was watching a 20/20 report about some of the Wall Street moguls looking for jobs and having serious problems finding anything. One man with two children took a job as a pizza delivery driver to create some cash flow, as he could not find a job. With the work force possibly improving, the level of the service might start to go up, as the caliber of help becomes individuals who can **Read, Think, and Reason.**

Principle 10: Just Step Over It...

The Bar of Expectations

Don't let the lowering of the expectations affect your standards of service. In working to connect all the dots in the Cosmic Cow Pie, you just have to accept some people will not live up the expectations you have and therefore you might just have to step over the bar to have balance and maintain your own focus.

Your Notes

Chapter Eleven

It's Not My Monkey

Sometimes we take on responsibility that is not ours!

Eleven

It's Not My Monkey

In life, sometimes we take on burdens that do not belong to us. Learn the concept of **It's Not My Monkey** and be free of a false sense of responsibility. Many times when people have complained to us, we jump right in and try to fix the situation for them.

When you accept someone else's monkey, the process tends to drain you emotionally. Tasks you are supposed to be working on are late and you have to work longer than expected to accomplish your goals for the day.

STOP TAKING ON OTHER PEOPLE'S MONKEYS!

✓   Learn how to say politely in a gentle soft voice, **"It's not my monkey."** When the individual leans in and inquires, "What did you say?" in a little louder voice repeat, **"It's not my monkey."** When the individual leans in again and questions, "What did you say?" respond in an even louder voice, **"It's not my**

monkey." When the person looks shocked, start yelling at the top of your lungs, **"It's not my monkey"** and they will **"Get It."** They will have learned that you are not going to take the responsibility or bail them out of something they should be doing.

Two of my friends demonstrated the Monkey principle I had shared with them the night before in Denver, Colorado. I was doing a presentation at an office and I needed to set up the computer with a projector so all in the room could see the web site. At the office, the Internet was not connecting. My friend's wife was looking to him to solve the problem. He looked at me and simply said, "It's not my office; I don't know why it's not working and **it's not my monkey**." He was right, but women being women, his wife was trying to help by getting her husband to figure it out. It really was not his monkey. He had learned the concept well! I found the office manager and she hooked it up and the situation was resolved.

A friend of our family had a Range Rover that had been to three repair shops over the last two months trying to find someone who could replace the engine. The young friend was the same age as my daughter and she needed a ride into Flagstaff to start at Northern Arizona University where my daughter attended school. I took it upon myself to try to help her out and let her borrow the car our daughter was going to be using when she arrived back home in a few days. It worked out that the young woman wanted a ride into Flagstaff from Williams, almost 30 miles each day for an extended period while her car was in the shop. It started out with the girls having each other as company but when the friend needed a ride for a night class, the arrangement started to become a burden.

I was the one who let her borrow our car until our daughter came back to town and needed it to drive to school. You see, I took on the monkey of the girl needing to get to school, and she did not even ask for help. I was actually feeding the monkey which bothered my daughter as she had to plan her day around the girl's needs and not her own. I gave my daughter a monkey she did not ask for. One day my daughter wanted to hang out with another friend and she told me clearly that this girl needing to go for a night class and use the car was "**not her monkey.**" I explained to her I had created this problem and asked if she would please help me out which at the same time would be helping the young woman. She agreed and I had learned my lesson: not to take on more monkeys at the expense of others.

Sometimes a parent will take on a child's monkey because it is easier to get it done themselves. A parent has a tendency to want to make life easier for the child instead of helping them become independent adults doing things for themselves. A friend of mine learned late in life that helping the kids was becoming a wedge between her husband and her because she was always stepping in to save the day. She would take the adult children's

> **Who's Your Monkey?**
>
> *Whisper quietly, "It's not my monkey,"*
> *Then a little louder, "It's not my monkey,"*
> *Then scream and rant, "It's not my monkey!"*

monkeys including grandchildren, and make them her own. As she learned to let her children and their families work on their own monkeys, she became less stressed and more balanced. Her husband was thrilled that she was letting go.

As an over achiever, many times a person may volunteer to help with new projects when they have a barrel of their own monkeys. It is OK to take on monkeys to help others; just be sure that you are taking them on because you want to do something nice for the other individual. Be aware not to take on monkeys that are not yours, as they can drown you if you are not careful.

Be prepared when you teach this concept to your family and friends, they will be happy to throw it back at you. Who's your monkey?

Principle 11: It's Not My Monkey

Determine which monkeys to keep and which monkeys to Kick to the Curb. This principle will help you stay balanced in the Cosmic Cow Pie. Do not accept the false responsibility of taking on another person's monkey.

Your Notes

Chapter Twelve

Stuff Our Parents Didn't Teach Us

Twelve

Stuff Our Parents Didn't Teach Us

It is hard for a parent to teach everything we will encounter in life, so some things we will learn on our own. Sharing some ideas might make for better balance in dealing with difficult circumstances and help us through the Cosmic Cow Pie of life.

The *Circle of Life*, an academy award-nominated song from Disney's 1994 animated film, THE LION KING, exemplifies how life plays out. In the movie, Simba is the lion cub who was supposed to inherit the kingdom. Rafika is a baboon who watches Simba as he grows and helps him with life's lessons after his father has passed. Rafika hits Simba over the head with a stick when he does not remember lessons he had learned in his life. It seems like we all need a Rafika to help us with remembering our lessons.

The first area I did not get lessons for was how to help or talk to someone when a loved one passed away. The first family member I remember passing was my Grandmother. I was about ten and the family left the children in other room so we did not hear any of the discussion. I can only remember my mother saying that if I wanted to remember my Gram the way she was, I should not look in the casket. To this day, I do not look inside the casket of anyone who has passed. It has been hard to understand what to say, or how to act, around people who are sad with their loss. I have learned to address the loss and fill the void with remembering all the love the individual who passed gave to the world. I then encourage others to think about the wonderful memories they

> *Circle of Life*
>
> *From the day we arrive on the planet*
> *And blinking, step into the sun*
> *There's more to be seen than can ever be seen*
> *More to do than can ever be done*
> *Some say eat or be eaten*
> *Some say live and let live*
> *But all are agreed as they join the stampede*
> *You should never take more than you give*
> *In the circle of life*
>
> **-Elton John and Tim Rice**

have that will last forever. We then talk about how love lives on with them every day.

Another area that was fuzzy for me was what to do and say when a friend learns of a terminal illness diagnosis. To be able to help and comfort the individual and his or her family is a skill everyone should learn. The first thing to do to help would be to physically go over and express your love and assure the family and the individual you are there for them and will help them in any way possible. They may say they do not need help so take some initiative and ask what kind of food would be good to bring to make things easier. Give them some ideas like chicken breasts, meatloaf, and spaghetti so they have choices. Ask them if they have other friends who are wanting to help and if they have a list of people with phone numbers so you could contact them and make a volunteer schedule to organize even some cleaning help. Do this, if and only if, they would like the help. The key point is to start the dialogue about helping and then step up to the plate and just do it.

I have a friend with a serious lung condition. She is a single parent and has no family living near her. When diagnosed, she realized that she needed a support group. She arranged a tea party with all of her friends to talk with them about the disease and what she would need. Her friends rallied, created a phone tree, and assigned duties to each person for laundry, babysitting, food delivery, prayer, and visitation. If you know someone who has a health condition you might want to open a conversation and ask them how you could best be a friend and what you could do to help them feel more cared for and loved.

I recently had a forty-five year old friend diagnosed with a stage four terminal situation and I was talking to her on the phone with all the love and positive affirmations I could offer. She let me know directly, "I cannot wait for the rest of my family and friends to be ready for me to move on." Her message came in loud and clear. She was changing her zip code and it did not matter if her family and I were ready. I was trying to be upbeat and be positive but she was ready to pass on and was helping me let go. I was grateful for the gift in being able to release her without being sad, as she was prepared and ready to move on.

When I was about 34, the wife of my husband's friend had a terminal diagnosis several months prior to our notification. I was horrified with the news, as I did not know what to say or how to act. The time ticked by and we had not gone to see her. Her husband called and told us she wanted to see us. I froze with the fear of not knowing what to say. My husband and I were finally going to see her and we ran into a terrible traffic jam. We turned around to go another day and we never made it to see her before she passed and the guilt still lives with me. I now know to embrace any person with a problem with love, kindness, understanding, and respect. I do not delay when I learn about the news.

✓ Know that the patient will lead conversation in the direction they want to go. If you are expressing love and listening for direction, you will do the right thing naturally.

Once you have wrapped your mind around the concept of how to help in a crisis you will be a wonderful addition of strength to your friends and family. When the call of a friend's passing comes in, as you are discussing the timing for family to arrive, determine on your own when they will need some easy-to-prepare food items. At this time, no one is really thinking clearly and certainly not about food. Most friends want to do something but again, they do not know what to do. If family is coming in, let your friend know you will go to the store and bring them some easy to fix lunch items and bring them right over. Make it easy on yourself and easy for them. Purchasing a fully cooked ham, having it sliced in sandwich style slices, along with bread, wraps, mustard, mayonnaise, lettuce, Swiss cheese, chips, pasta salad or cole slaw, pickles, fruit, some chocolate, cookies and a selection of soda and tea is a wonderful gift to take over as family arrives. As the time goes on, they will receive many casserole type dishes but this gift really helps at the beginning of the planning process and your friends will remember your quick response in their time of need.

Transitioning into a lighter subject of things our parents did not teach us is how to let go as children go off to college. Our children's generation is so different from when we left home it is again an experience which is hard to accept. One of the best things I did was to read a book on letting go and one chapter made it so much easier for me. The book encouraged the parents and student to role-play about leaving for college. Every time our daughter went out with her friends from about the middle of the last semester in her senior year of high school, we would say, "this is it, we are saying goodbye at college and things will never be the same." We would cry and hug and get over the hurt very quickly as we knew it was a dress rehearsal for real life, we were just practicing and she would be home later in the evening. The high school chapter does end in everyone's life and your children will be starting life as independent adults.

We practiced the parting feelings so often that when it came time to say goodbye at Whittier College in California, the event did not have tears and we were all happy the new chapter was underway. There was absolutely no separation anxiety at that particular moment. The adjustment will take time to accept but the actual parting is much easier after you practice.

Principle 12: Stuff Our Parents Didn't Teach Us

Thinking about how to handle death and sickness in advance will help you get through those times in life where you need to help others and be in control. Connecting the dots in the Cosmic Cow Pie is a lot easier as you apply the principles of the book to achieve more balance.

Your Notes

Chapter Thirteen

You Can't Get To Carnegie Hall If You Don't Practice!

Play It Out

Thirteen

You Can't Get to Carnegie Hall If You Don't Practice! Play It Out

Play It Out is a concept that can save you hours of potential stress and put you in a position of power when situations change in your life. Learning this principle is another life skill, which makes you stronger as the winds of change blow. Role-playing is not something everyone can do or enjoys. It is, however, a way to see how events might play out in a specific situation. You can do this in your mind and only you will know what is going on in your personal decision making process.

By **Playing It Out**, you will be prepared for events that you know are going to happen in the future. We all have bridges we have to go over as time moves on with

> *The more I practice, the luckier I get.*
>
> *-Gary Player, professional golfer and three time Masters Champion*

occurrences in our lives. To make the journey easier, the principle of **Playing It Out** can help make the result more palatable to accept. If you can process the inevitable now, you will be spared negative energy and you will be able to understand the event in a nano second, moving on to more productive things in your life, thereby removing stress and working towards balance in the Cosmic Cow Pie of life.

✓ To **Play It Out and Practice**, look at the worst it can be and then figure out what you can do about it. Once you have come to terms with the remedy, you can go forward and do what you need to do if the situation arises.

Using the **Play It Out** principle during the 2008 Presidential election, I played it out in my mind, acknowledging there would be a winner and a loser. Not everyone would be happy with the results but we all had to come to grips with the outcome and go forward. In any event, one person was not going to remedy the economic and environmental mess quickly. As I practiced accepting the possible scenarios, I came to grips with the fact that the change was going to be painful no matter what happened and we would all have to participate to make the necessary adjustments. In **Playing It Out**, there would be one winner and one loser. The people who were unhappy would have to **Build a Bridge and Get Over It**.

To take this principle to a different level, one that you might use every day, consider the example that involves time management and **Playing It Out**. My husband wanted to drive to Flagstaff to get new tires on Monday. Flagstaff is 30 miles from our home and, of course, 30 miles back. Utilizing the **Playing It Out** principle, I was thinking that we needed to go to Flagstaff for a City Council meeting on Tuesday so why would he go to Flagstaff two days in a row? My thoughts were to go early on Tuesday so we just made one trip to Flagstaff. Our daughter was going to school at Northern Arizona University so he had arranged to meet her while he waited to get the tires changed. I did not want to make a big deal about the arrangements he already made, as he had just gotten off the phone and set the appointment. When he was done, I asked him if it would be possible to do it on Tuesday when we had to go into town anyway. He was not a happy camper and told me "no," he had just made the appointment. I played it out for him explaining we were going into town on Tuesday so if we just went in early we could get the tires changed and have dinner before the Council meeting killing three birds with one trip. I then told him that all he had to do was to call the tire company and change the day and the time. After a few angry moments, he decided that might be a better idea. Did we have conflict? Yes, we did. Did we resolve it? Yes, we did. Did we learn from playing things out and then being flexible, that there is a way to use time and gas money efficiently? Yes, we did.

Basic time management skills are of the upmost importance with the concept of practicing an event and playing it out. When you are trying to arrange with others for a social gathering or a meeting, you need to factor in all the plans you have scheduled prior to the meeting and then factor in the time to get to the location of the new event. You must anticipate a fudge factor with time for traffic problems and for mistakes in finding an address. The Internet is good for getting turn-by-turn directions, but remember, sometimes the directions are wrong! It is always wise to confirm with someone the exact directions before jumping in with your Internet map.

I had an opportunity to **Play Out** the entire testimony of a court hearing in front of a video judge when my Real Estate client had a complaint against a builder and we had to present the case directly to the camera and the Registrar of Contractors. We did have a training video, so we watched it several times and knew the process. I wrote questions, which when answered, presented the facts of the case. I practiced with my client just as an attorney would question a witness. We did this three times and we thought about what the outcome would be and how the judge would react. This Practice took six hours and when we arrived at the hearing, we felt prepared for anything that might happen. We entered early and were calm, cool, and collected as we had **Practiced and Played Out** all possible endings to the hearing. We played out the results including the worst-case scenario where the judge ruled the issue was not something he could handle as the Registrar of Contractors and would have to go to a Civil Court. We had been waiting for this day in court for over 18 months so that specific result would not have felt good, but we were prepared. We mentally prepared for the cost of losing which included paying attorney fees and court costs. We knew what she would accept as a settlement and what she was willing to do if the settlement paid out in monthly installments.

Because the attorney had provided the documentation prior to the hearing, we knew what he was going to say. This was the funniest part of the **Practicing** because the attorney had documentation for the wrong property. We **Played it Out** thinking the attorney could be using it as a precedent, which had been completed on another home the builder had constructed, or he just plain made a mistake. We laughed for 15 minutes on the **Practiced** result with the possibility the respondent to the complaint brought the wrong documentation.

The hearing was on a Monday at 8:15 so we did not have time to be at the wrong place to check in at 8:00. The documentation she had did not include an address of the hearing so we needed to figure this out on a Sunday. I decided to call the court in Phoenix just to see if there was a recording on the video hearings. Lo and behold, a person answered the phone and knew where we needed to go. That one call saved a sleepless night and stressful morning, hoping we were going to the right location for the hearing.

We arrived almost 30 minutes early as we had extra time built into our plan. When we arrived, we had time to gather ourselves together, neatly organize our documentation, and be ready for the video hearing. The builder called into the office at 8:10 not knowing where he was supposed to show up. He looked stressed to the max as he entered the room. He had less than two minutes to be ready for the judge to come on the video screen. The attorney asked the buyer if she had received the documentation he sent and she told him she had received it on Friday before she flew in from Wisconsin. At that point, she let him know the information was on the wrong house. The attorney about fell through the floor and looked at the builder for help. It was too late as the hearing was about to start.

When the judge came on the screen, he asked if we had tried to settle the complaint and the buyer indicated the attempt at settlement had ended after filing the complaint. The attorney asked for 15 minutes to try to work something out and the buyer agreed. At that point, all our preparations were the perfect defense to their disorganized mess. The best it could be was **Playing Out**. The builder and the attorney had created a case on the wrong house. The builder and the attorney had to go out of the room to talk at least four times. They had not played anything out. The judge kept coming in and the attorney would ask for 15 more minutes. They wanted to buy more time and reschedule the hearing later. At that point, I stepped in to say, "What property did you think you were coming to this hearing about? You received the information for the past 18 months and you showed up today with wrong documentation. The answer is no extension, the buyer has flown in from Wisconsin, had to miss work and this is her day in court and she is prepared to go forward even if you are not."

The builder and the attorney realized they had just been steam rolled and were going to lose. They came back with a cash settlement less than the amount owed. The buyer had **Played It Out** and of course the answer was "no." They came back with another plan and asked if we wanted to go outside and talk. We did only for a few minutes and again, the answer was "no." They continued to come up with ideas and then we did not have to go out. We indicated we had already discussed some of the possibilities they were suggesting and none of them worked except him paying the entire amount he owed. You see, we had **Practiced** as if we were going to Carnegie Hall and we had **Played Out** every single scenario so were prepared to be in control during the entire event. If the builder did not pay, he would lose his license. If he goes bankrupt, the Recovery fund from the state protects the buyer. The result was a fantastic win situation for the buyer who prepared for every possible outcome by **Practicing and Playing It Out**.

Principle 13: You Can't Get To Carnegie Hall If You Don't Practice! Play It Out

Apply the principle of playing out an event you know is going to happen to be prepared for all possible outcomes. You will relieve stress and experience a sense of calmness in going through the situation. Practice, Practice, Practice everything you undertake in life. Accept the fact you have to Practice to be perfect and you have to start at the beginning to learn.

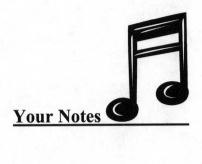

Your Notes

Chapter Fourteen

Managing the Mess

Fourteen

Managing the Mess

Managing the Mess of flying obstacles in the Cosmic Cow Pie is a skill everyone can use in the changing times we live in. Sometimes, the light at the end of the tunnel seems to be a freight train coming at us. The economic freight train is running over almost every family in one way or another. No one seems to be exempt from the path.

In early 2007, I came to the realization everyone in our family could be feeling the effects soon and we needed to have a family plan. My 24-year-old daughter living in Maui had spent eight months working her dream job in public relations at a high-end cooking store, booking Celebrity Chefs and orchestrating programs to bring in customers. When she was visiting my husband and me in Arizona on a surprise trip for her birthday, I shared my vision of the direction of the economy. I suggested that she needed to be aware of the fact she lived on an island and if the economic wave started to rise in Hawaii she needed to pack up and get out of there before she drowned. She laughed a little but assured me she would be prepared if she was run over or the tide was rising.

My husband and I went to Maui for the winter in January of 2009. We had only been in Maui for about three weeks when my daughter and I were discussing the chapter in this book on goal setting and always having a **Plan B**. We talked about how people need to plan in specific time segments such as a weekly plan, a monthly plan, a one-year plan, a five-year plan, up to an exit plan.

Our daughter lost her dream job and the store closed as the economy took a nosedive. She had been struggling with finding another job that paid as much as she had been making. None of the hotels was hiring and many people were working three and four-day workweeks just to keep their jobs. She played the numbers out and determined if she stayed on Maui with even a two thousand dollar a month job she would not have any savings to buy a home or get ahead in five years and she would be at the same place she was now. A light had gone off in her head and she saw the **"I Get It"** button clearly. She went home and talked with her boyfriend and they decided they needed to sell everything and move back to the mainland. It was literally overnight they decided, and all the things to accomplish before the move were suddenly daunting. The race against time with unemployment running out, no job, in the middle of the Pacific, was a huge burden.

I realized that she might need some help. Having moved from the islands once before, I knew how much there was to coordinate: determining a date to leave, giving notice at the apartment, buying a plane ticket, and selling all their belongings. I thought I could help with some organizational skills and then let them carry out the physical plan. Parents do tend to take on the monkeys of their children and sometimes it helps the child, and sometimes it keeps them from growing on their own. In this case, we shared the monkey and I taught my daughter some new skills that will assist her later in life.

The project was overwhelming to me so outlining **Plan A** and **Plan B** was going to be important. As a master of **Managing the Mess**, I understood completely how big this mess was and how we needed to get right on top of it before her unemployment ran out and she would be figuratively sinking on the island.

My daughter started by writing down all the projects and tasks looming before her. The biggest problem was going to be selling all the furniture and belongings they did not want to ship back to the mainland, as it would be too expensive. The separation anxiety created by selling all their belongings evaporated by looking at the cost to ship things back to the mainland. It made more sense to sell everything and start over than to spend money they did not have to ship things back. I had collected Real Estate magazines about current listed properties. I asked my daughter to go through all the books and find the e-mail addresses of the Realtors. I told her we did not need a name just the e-mail address and I would send out a mass e-mail to the Realtors about all the things she would be selling. She needed to make a list on a Microsoft word document including everything she needed to sell, and put the price she paid for it and the price she would sell it for now. She then needed to take pictures of each item one at a time so we could show potential buyers what she had for sale. My daughter is an over achiever when she wants to be and the job was completed the next day so I went to work creating a photo gallery album online at Kodak.com. The picture album had an assigned URL or Internet address so we could copy the link address and insert it directly into the e-mail to the Real Estate agents and Craig's List, providing a quick advertising solution.

In a perfect world, she really did not want to deal with selling things one at a time and preferred to sell it as a package. I created an e-mail describing the fact she would sell all the items for a discounted price if someone purchased everything. There were wonderful deals on her list. For example, a new queen bed that she paid $1,035 listed for $375, creating a potential money maker if someone bought the bed and then resold it to make more money. The package with all the items was $2,800, and she was willing to discount the grouping for $2,500. The original value was well over $8,000 so we felt this concept might work. I sent out an e-mail to the Real Estate agents indicating she would wait for one week to find a buyer for the package but would take individual names on each item in case she did not find someone. I put the information on Craig's List with the list of items and the link to the pictures. We started getting e-mails immediately and had over sixty names on the waiting list for the individual items. The night before she was prepared to start selling items individually, a buyer called wanting all the items and would wait to pick them up until she was ready to leave. We handled the monkeys in the mess. The best part of the advertising was the fact it was all free and done in cyber space.

✓ To **Manage the Mess** in the Cosmic Cow Pie, it takes focus and dedication to the goal. Identify all the tasks to finish in a certain circumstance, and then create a plan for each item describing exactly what you want. In the big scheme of life, you might just get what you want. Even when it seems like too much to accomplish, if you break it down one item at a time, you can complete the task.

My daughter and her boyfriend sold all their belongings and were on their way within thirty-one days of deciding to move from the Island. An incredible amount of work occurred in a short time but they did it with planning and moved on to the next chapter in their lives. My small part was to implement the advertising and coordinate the information. They worked the plan doing everything that needed to be completed physically.

Another **Mess needing some Management** help was for a friend of mine who had trouble managing her money. In 1999, my friend had just moved into a new home and was planning new drapes and furniture when her roommate of eleven years committed his last act of domestic violence with her and she had him arrested. She called me in her hour of desperation to come and help. Her roommate owed his half of all of the moving expenses and down payment charged on her credit cards. She was now stuck with $30,000 in debt and down half of the household monthly income. She was in a panic about how to pay all of the bills and survive. The only solution she could think of was to sell the house. In the midst of her anguish, her 9-year-old son came home from school and told her he needed $4.00 for a field trip the next day. She did not even have the $4.00 to give him. She started to envision them going to live in a homeless shelter. She called me for help and I told her I would be right over.

Within five minutes, I was at her front door. We sat down at the kitchen table. I firmly took control of the situation and asked to see all of the bills. I helped sort through which bills to pay immediately, and which bills

> *What would you think if I sang out of tune*
> *Would you stand up and walk out on me?*
> *Lend me your ears and I'll sing you a song*
> *and I'll try not to sing out of key*
> *Oh, I get by with a little help from my friends*
>
> *-The Beatles*

could wait. We had a serious discussion about the difference between need and want, and decided that the bedroom set and new drapes needed to be on the back burner and the old furniture and drapes would have to suffice. The cable package needed to change to basic, as she needed to count every penny. I helped her make a budget, and made her promise to stick to it. Then, I asked for three envelopes. She labeled them "groceries," "gas" and "incidentals" like field trips. I taught her to put cash in each envelope at the beginning of the month based on what was in the budget for that item, and when it was gone, it was gone. My friend still uses the system to this day and she taught her son the same method.

My friend tells me that she still remembers the day she learned to take control of her own financial situation. She needed the structure and no-nonsense approach to **Manage her Mess**. We approached it as a problem to solve which is what we did.

My friend had this to say, "After Carra left that day, under the placemat on my kitchen table, I found $100 cash. I cried. I had never expected a helping hand. It got me through the month, and my son was able to go on his field trip. That act of kindness propelled me to make the changes I needed to make, and I have since paid it forward to someone else in need. With financial help from my family, I kept my house, got out of debt within three years and have control over my finances, still always weighing if I need, or merely want, something before I purchase it. This lesson has made a huge difference in balance and focus in my life."

Many times in life, we experience messes that give us pits in our stomachs, and the anxiety seems so high it appears we are never going to get through a particular circumstance. It seems like there are just too many obstacles or cow pies flying around in the universe to be able to have balance. By applying the Manage the Mess principle, you can get through anything, one step at a time.

Principle 14: Managing the Mess

We all have messes and it is easy to look the other way. Focus on the solution and not the mess. Think about the resolution to the problem in increments, baby steps, and work toward the desired result. The dots do come together in the Cosmic Cow Pie when you Practice the 14 Principles in this book to help focus and create balance in your life.

Your Notes

Chapter Fifteen

Connecting the Dots
and
Rules for Life

Fifteen

Connecting the Dots and Rules for Life

After reading this book I hope, dear reader, the dots are starting to connect in the Cosmic Cow Pie as you embrace the 14 Principles to help you focus and create balance in your life, free of stress. Do not worry about the things you cannot change. Learn to process information and be prepared to move on. Concentrate on **Read, Think, and Reason**. Be sure to read everything and reason from a position of power, which is the knowledge you already have. Do not get caught up in **Drama** of new ideas or your friend's lives. Keep on track, **Play Things Out** and always have a **Plan B**. **Practice, Practice, and Practice** whatever you undertake. Remember not to take on additional **Monkeys** and tame the few you own. You can **Connect the Dots** in the Cosmic Cow Pie to focus and have a balanced life. Watch for a children's workbook coming out to teach your children the concepts in this book and prepare them for handling their own experiences in the Cosmic Cow Pie of life. www.CosmicCowPie.com.

The Principles in Cosmic Cow Pie actually started from the "Rules for Life" I created when my stepdaughters were in their teens. My youngest daughter knew from the time she could speak about the first three "rules." She knew when we went into to a store "Rule Number One" applied. She would exclaim, "Mom, I know Rule Number One is in effect." Share these rules and have fun doing it!

1. You don't always get what you want
2. Sometimes you have to do things you don't want to do
3. Life is not always fair
4. You must be patient
5. Always have a Plan B
6. Always do the right thing
7. Forgive means to forget
8. Know who's your monkey
9. Know when to listen
10. Know when to stop

Rule Number 10 is now in effect. Know when to stop!

I Get It!

For more information about the upcoming Children's workbook following the **COSMIC COW PIE...CONNECTING THE DOTS** principles:

info@CosmicCowPie.com or www.CosmicCowPie.com.